Pratbimb: Transcendence

A Collections of Poems: Reflections of My Soul

Atul Pandita Lifeographer

BookLeaf Publishing
India | USA | UK

Made with ❤ on the BookLeaf Publishing Platform
www.bookleafpub.in
www.bookleafpub.com

Dedication

Dedciated to each and every soul, that I have come across my lifetime on this Earth. Thanks a gazillion for the endless inspiration.

Thanks to the Almighty for this life. Eternally grateful.

Preface

A Photographer by both passion and profession, I call myself, a "Lifeographer"...I also call myself an accidental poet. Ever since my first encounter with a Kodak DC 215 Zoom camera, almost 20
years ago...I have thoroughly engaged myself in drawing life portraits with the help of my ever so faithful shutterbug. Portraits full of life...full of positivity... portraits teeming
with infinite energy. Portraits that are like a beautiful poem...
that, which transcend the space time continuum. I also wrote some words and phrases trying to capture the raw emotions of each portrait that I created...which eventually took the shape of some sort of poetry...18 poems to be exact. I now, share this interesting amalgam with you all through this book. Hopefully, I shall continue to write more material in the visible future...and share iterations through similar forms with you all.

Till then...

Have a good read!!

Acknowledgements

"No one who achieves success does so without acknowledging the help of others. The wise and confident acknowledge this help with gratitude."

--Alfred North Whitehead--

Chapter. 1. Life Journeys

These long and twisty roads I constantly ride,
All of my frustrations...all of pain, I successfully hide.
I load up my truck and set myself on that long and
rugged path,
As those hot winds and that unforgiving sun...unleash
upon me
their seething wrath.
And yet, I move ahead...un-phased and unhurt,
As all of that muck...that sweat begin to stain my shirt.
However, I shall fight all elements with utmost grit...I
shall
survive,
As, Lady Luck came down to me and extended me a high
five.
And, so, I shall continue my endeavours and immerse
myself in
that Light of God,
I shall strive to eliminate each and every negativity...each
and
every odd.

For, I shan't stop fighting...I shall not, at any cost...stop,
I shall defeat all the lackdaisicality of my very life...I shall succeed
and come out on top....
....I shall definitely succeed ohh my dearest friends and come out on
top!!
For, I am a Lifeographer...I paint portraits of this ohh so beautiful
life,
With beauty, serenity and peace it is very much rife.
These journeys...
I shall always remember,
Filling my stone-cold heart with warmth and love...thus, making it
tender. These moments...these figments, I pluck with the help of
my
aperture,
Spreading happiness and positivity is an integral part of my
nature. I look at them...they look at me...and, I click
And therefore, make time with my camera...eternally stick.
'Coz, I am a Lifeographer...I paint portraits of this ohh so beautiful life,
Life...that, which beauty,

serenity and peace, is very much rife...........
That, which beauty, serenity and peace, is very much rife.

Chapter. 2. Tamanna

Hello Sir!
Remember me?
Yes...No??
Well, I do indeed know you...but you don't know me??
Well...if you
would kindly spare a few minutes of your precious
time... I'll tell
you who I really am.
Don't worry Sir, I shan't take much time.
But... Where should I start? I do not know...ahh yes... I
am a
human being...just like you,
And, like you I live and breathe...inside my chest beats a
soft and
a vulnerable heart. My form is not my choice...this is
something I
did not want to be,
Like you Sir, I had dreams... aspirations...a gazillion
things I
wanted to do...and a gazillion places I wanted to see.

However, I do not know how I ended up here... standing in front of
you...bearing the brunt of both your ire and your ridicule,
Becoming the butt of all your lewd jokes and abuses...I saw myself
being reduced to mere useless tool.
And then you took off in your rocket ship... throwing dust in my
face...running away, when that signal turned green,
You quickly let go of that horrendous monster you had just been.
You forgot that you had just murdered me with your words...you
had killed off my beautiful and tender soul,
You had created inside me...with your sneering and hate-filled
eyes...an infinite and a dark hole.
Despite all of this, however, I chose to bless you with His powers,
I asked Him to forgive you...and bring in your life endless health
filled and prosperous showers.
I asked Him to take away all your pain...taking away countless
miseries and disappointments,
I hoped and prayed...that my horrendous face...may

never come in
front of you ever again!!
And yet...today, you stand in front of me...your eyes
filled with a
little bit of shame and lots of remorse,
Well...Sir, this is what I call poetic justice...this is what I
call
destiny, of course!!!
And Sir, just so to let you know...my name is Tamanna
and yes, I
belong to the so called, "Third Gender"
But that doesn't change the fact that, like you, I am a
human
being...and, just like you, a heart beats inside me that is
soft and
tender.
You may leave now...as, I've finished whatever I wanted
to say,
Nothing more to add...nothing more that is left inside
me,
I do hope though, that my words...my voice...be inside of
you and
forever
and ever...they may stay.......................................
...My words...my voice...be
inside of you and forever and ever...they may stay!!

Chapter. 3. Vishal

My first ever canvas portrait was of this brilliant kid...eight years ago.

A soul of the lively streets of our beautiful National Capital,
He waves at me, whenever I pass him at the traffic signal.
Where he can be seen selling everything from water sprays to
balloons, Or maybe balancing a 100 or something flutes, of which
one he holds in his mouth...to play some random tunes.
A couple of weeks ago, there was a break in this routine when he
stopped me and asked me to give him a print of his portrait.
As I didn't have it at the time, I...gave him a box full of chocolate
donuts filled up in a paper crate. His smile said it all. Also, I

promised to return to give him his portrait.
Next day, 5.30 PM...he sees my car at the signal...his heavy balloons
almost lifting him in the air because of their weight and sheer numbers...must be a 100 of them.
Knocks on my window and I hand over the portrait all rolled up...an
ever increasing audience of kids (comprising of his street brothers
and sisters) gather around him as he unveils his treasured gem!!
A loud "ohhhhhh" accompanied by shrills of laughter is followed as
soon as he sees himself in that picture. The shrill however, is not
from him but from his audience.
They are besides themselves seeing their hero as a portrait. He's their superstar...
their hero...the centre of their worldly existence.
They're jumping excitedly prompting their extended families to leave everything
and see what he holds in his hands.
And then, there's this fellow...standing there and, staring at his picture while
others are playing their happiness bands!!
He's not used to this kind of attention. He sees his face...yes...in other's windows

or maybe their rear view mirrors other's windows or maybe their rear view mirrors.
But not like this...this is new for him...this gives him continuous shivers!
Me asking his name...where he lives and all. Others know him as just another street urchin. He doesn't know what to do...except keep admiring himself in that picture along with his kin.
Suddenly...he looks at me and through unspoken words asks me to click him. I oblige...putting my camera into action. I click as many shots as I can capture.
He doesn't say a word...except staring happily into my aperture!
I am sure his heart has converted into an F1 engine. On the outside though, he's got a saintly calm about him...breaking into a smile when prompted by his fans.
He then starts to pose...yep...he's a poser alright...while my camera, across his expressions...vigorously pans.
Finally, gripping himself...he comes to thank me shaking my hand violently.
He wants to say something through this hoarse yet beautiful voice...but before

he can finish...the signal turns green and I am forced to move by the impatient
lot behind me.
He runs behind my truck...waving goodbye and sending some flying kisses for good
measure. I do the same through my open window.
He then stops as I pull away...gradually disappearing from my rear view
mirror...the last image of him being lost between his swelled up audience...his fans.
His name is Vishal and he is not just a street urchin...this fellow.
And so, we're the best of friends and shall, always be...we shall be religiously
continuing with our daily routine.
So yeah...his name is Vishal and he is not just a street urchin...this fellow...to meet
him, you all, I am sure...are pretty keen...............
..............To meet him, I am sure, you all are pretty keen.

Chapter. 4. Jeevan

There is this life...this brilliantly beautiful tide...that I
constantly
ride,
My thoughts, emotions and my wishes...I always tend to
hide.
There is a milieu of earthen mortals that surround
me...they
come across as unbelievably strange,
Their moods, their whims and also, their very faces...they
seem to
change.
They are your friends...your well-wishers...your
everything...at
the very start,
And then they hit you with a hammer...they begin to rip
you
apart.
They dismantle your self-respect...they eat into your
soul,
They make sure that they suck every ounce of willpower

from
within
you...and then, bury you in a dark and a deep hole.
And then after a while...when the dust sets upon the earth...they
do turn around and come back,
Yeah...that is what they do...they often display their very own
trademark knack.
Flabbergasted by seeing me alive...living my life...on that brilliantly beautiful tide,
That I always tend to sit upon...I always tend to ride.
I look at them...and welcome them with arms open...and then, I
simply ask them to go away,
They've played enough with my soul and therefore, cannot stay.
They tell me that I need them...without them my life shan't have
any warmth...it shall be as cold as a stone,
But they do not know...that now I do not need them...He is standing
right beside me and therefore, I am no longer alone.
So, therefore, let me ride that beautiful tide...let me move you all
aside...as on that brilliant wave of hope I jump and slide,
And let me untie those beautiful emotions...yes...those

very
emotionsthat I can no longer hide...
...can no longer hide.
For, my Life is beautiful...it is indeed very new,
It is so brilliant...those who understand it are only a few.
She' s asking me to get up and live.
Sleeping in my cosy bed...is something that she does not want...she needs our 100%...that we need to give.
So... let me live...let me live and thank Him for every day that He
grants me to live.

Chapter. 5. Lifeographer

These faces...these lives...that I paint,
They're so silent...so weak...so very faint.
And yet, they leave an indelible mark on my soul,
Those seething eyes...tend to burn me from within...they
create
an infinite hole.
These are attributes that I can never ever forget,
Freezing them in time...is what I love...is what I never
regret.
I have the ability to find happiness...in this world that,
which
is filled with sadness,
That beautiful quantum of solace...that hides away in all
of that
ruckus...all of that madness........
......It is this very maddening life that I constantly ride,
All of my frustrations...all of pain, I successfully hide.
I load up that caravan, and set myself on that long and
rugged
path,

As those hot winds and that unforgiving sun...unleash
upon me
their seething wrath.
Yet, I move ahead...unphased and unhurt,
As all of that muck...that sweat begin to stain my shirt.
However, I fight all those elements with utmost grit...
their
antics I successfully survive,
As, Lady Luck comes down to me and extends me a high
five.
And, so, I shall continue my endeavours and immerse
myself in
that Light of God,
I shall strive to eliminate each and every negativity...each
and
every odd.
For, I am a Lifeographer...portraits of life is what I paint,
My existence...well, it is exciting, positive and definitely
very
quaint!!!
Power to this beautiful world...power to every human
being...
Live your life...live your dreams...and stop never ever!!

"Light up the darkness":: Bob Marley

Chapter. 6. Sky Dance

There is a brilliant fire in those skies,
A perfect medicine for my injured soul and my ohh so sullen eyes.
I lift up my head...awestruck by that beautiful golden light,
My mouth wide open...as I take in that superbly magnificent
sight.
This very light...this ohh so positive aura...fills my heart with
love,
As both day and night dance across that horizon...hand in glove.
Higher and higher they rise...those wonderful flames,
Giving the impression that God's own Angels are leaving their
prints...
writing their own names.
Seeing all of this beauty...
I cannot help but open up my heart and cry,

For God's love is being showered upon me...therefore,
I cannot stop those tears no matter how hard I try.
A new hope...a new energy comes along with each and every golden
ray,
Promising me that His love, His kindness and His blessings are
hear to stay.......... And that, alas!!! all of my pain...all of my sorrow
shall be permanently wiped away...and, that tomorrow shall be a
brighter and a prettier day!!!!
All in all... A blessed human being...to have been able to witness
this beautiful sunset,
An ethereal colouring on that sky high canvas...something that I
shall never forget.
A brilliant melange of taking the shape of a beautifully glimmering,
warm and a wonderful fire,
May it never ever die down...is my one and only desire.

Chapter. 7. Sreshthata

In your arms we come...take us in and never let us go,
We feel at peace...at home...for reasons we do not
understand...reasons we can never know.
You are beautiful...you are holy...you are sincere and you
are
really very sweet,
We all feel very happy whenever and wherever we meet.
We pray for a long and an abundant life...we pray for
your
health,
You are the Almighty's beautiful gift to us all...you are
our true
and brilliant wealth.
Your air we breathe, your food we eat and your waters
we drink,
Our fate prior to your sudden death, is something I do
not wish
fathom... something I cannot think.
We ask for your forgiveness...we know that we are very
much at

fault,
We beg of you never to stop showering your love and
your
blessings...we beg of you, to keep on growing...an aspect
that shall
never ever halt.
For, we shall all die...if you bid us goodbye,
We shan't be living a long and a serene life...no matter
how much
we
fight...no matter how hard we try.
Therefore, allow us, Ohh Mighty Mother...give us one
more
chance to live,
We shall never disappoint you... peace and satisfaction to
you...we
shall always give.
We shall pay homage to you... respect you today and
every
future day and age,
We shall make you happy, peaceful...we shall certainly
eliminate
your
rage.
We are your children, our dearest and beautiful Mother,
we wish
for to you to live a billion years...may you forever last,

And together, we may take our bleak future and turn it into a

brilliant and a memorable past................................

....................................For we shall take our bleak future and turn it

into a vibrant, memorable and brilliant past.

Chapter. 8. Flight

It is...within these beautiful clouds...that I can see my
final
resting place, A destination that excites me
limitlessly...sets my
heart up on a mad race. A place where I see the end of all
my
sorrow...all of the worldly madness.Where I can finally
bury that
old hatchet...and, get rid of that unending
sadness.Where...I shall
be finally be able to live again... Shall finally be able to
live all over
again. And, a destination that will finally end all of of my
grief...all
of that pain.
It does not matter if I fall,I am human, after all.
I would keep on trying,
Until, I am aloft and am flying.
My strength is exceptional and large,
As unyielding as a big and a strong barge.

For, I am like a bird who wishes to fly,
A being, yearning to touch the sky.
I need all the peace and the freedom,
That, which is found in God's very Own Heavenly Kingdom
And, alas...when I do take that beautiful and wonderful flight,
I shall vow to bring an end to all of my negativities...my woes...I
shall forever eliminate my plight. Only then, I shall swoop down
towards that ground...deciding to finally land,
When that hot and seething lava...has cooled down and turned into
silky sand.

Chapter. 9. Timelines

I am a human...if you failed to notice just in case,
For you I am someone without a name...someone with just a face.
I earn my living...I earn my bread,
I ensure that my children aren't starving when they go to bed. I
spend hours standing beneath that Sun,
Watching you and your families having fun. You look at me with
disdain,
Failing to recognize and understanding my pain. You don't want to
buy whatever I sell,
At least give me some water...it is hot as hell. But then again, I
forget that I am just another man without a name,
A life without any direction or for that matter any aim.
You see, Time...well it has left indelible furrows on my life,
Carving out silhouettes of emotions in the soul with an

invisible

knife.

Shadows falling on my face...darkness behind,

which I hide my emotions,

Tears, whenever they may fall...can create unending

oceans.

And, yet I contain these raging tornadoes...these

volcanoes inside

me,

And, make sure that it is my lifeless face...is the only

attribute

visible to you...the only attribute that you can see... The

only

attribute that you can see.

Still, I shall stand here and earn my bread,

And ensure that my children shan't starve before going

to

bed...shan't starve before going to bed.

Chapter. 10. Varchasva

In my hand...my very own life I hold,
My age number reads 41...and so, I am certainly not very
old. I
am highly optimistic about my future,
I am very positive about the whole thing...as being
positive is an
integral part of my nature.
Yes, I've had quite a few road blocks and some dead ends,
The path that I tread has got its share of potholes...and, a
lot
of unnecessary bends. But still, on this very path...I
continue to
move along,
Hopping and skipping merrily...I keep singing that very
beautiful
song. A song that to me...Lord Almighty has thoroughly
taught,
The very song with, which all of my negativities...I have
successfully
fought. And, it is a song...that I will and shall always

remember,
From the very first day of January to the last of day of December.
For, What I hold in my very own hand,
Is neither the wind, water nor is it sand. It is in fact my life...-
gifted to me my the Almighty God,
I am intrigued by way you look at it...your behaviour, I find
extremely odd. For, it is not for you that I live my life...it is very
much for me,
It has all the qualities...all the attributes...the ones, which I
hold...the ones that you can see. And, yes...it may appear to you as
a portrait in black and white,
It doesn't matter to me...as long as there that beautiful and
brilliant Light.
So, stay away...as far as you possibly can,
Your views and opinions bother me...them, I do not need...of them
I am not really a fan. For, I am an eagle...I am born to fly far
above the ground,
So, have a good life my dear friends...see you around...

Have a good
life my dearest friends...see you around.

Chapter. 11. Lockdown

What is this strange... tomultous...and boundless
calamity that has seemingly spread?
A little grief, a little sorrow it has brought... a little
gloom, it has quietly shed!
This hour of grief does not seem to pass...
This twilight refuses to fade, alas.
Time itself feels as though it has become a little
stagnant... a little flayed,
Life as though has become frozen, unmoved...a little
off...a little delayed.
All words, all talks, are caught in between...
Lingering there and then, where they have always been.

But...tomorrow, a new day shall arrive as the Sun shall
return once more,
Bringing with it countless wondrous rays of brilliance
and also, positivity in store.
This endless sorrow, this shadowed night,
It shall banish forever and ever with its brilliant and
beautiful light!

And once again joy will walk with us like a long lost
friend...who has come back to us...who is very dear,
And these chains of calamity, sorrow and
helplessness...this very friend of ours...shall make forever
disappear!

For together we shall make this world ohh so
beautiful...ohh so bright,
With firm resolve and sincerity...we shall move ahead
together...towards that very eternal light!
Step by step, side by side...we shall always tread,
Toward a new and radiant era ahead.........
.........Toward a new and radiant era ahead!!

Chapter. 12. Nomad

Who am I? Well...I am a nomad,
There is nothing that I do not have...yet am I am not
content
with my life...
I am a bit sad. I am an ethereal soul...
I am on the lookout for love...seeking harmony,
I cannot seem to find them..
despite the fact I have all the worldly comforts...
despite all that money.
This world that I live in...is full of lies and deceit,
People disguised as my well wishers...
ready to sweep me off my feet. I need to protect myself...
I need to end this all,
Else I shan't be able to survive...I shall definitely fall.
There is however still a small possibility, that I shall
these
missing attributes...there is still hope,
For there are many a unexplored avenues of my life...I
need to
look into...there is a lot of scope.

You see...I am an ethereal being...a beautiful soul,
And when I do find there elements...these brilliant attributes...
I shall be fully complete...I shall be whole........ Shall be fully
complete...
shall definitely be whole.

Chapter. 13. Pratibha

What we see in others and what they see in us...is,
essentially
the same.
Life as we know it, is no more than a beautiful game.
We carry those beautiful dreams...
brilliant aspirations, in our gleaming eyes.
Allowing others to peek inside our heart and our soul...
to seperate the truth from the lies.
There is more to us than just black and white.
We are the bearers of a Holy Entity...the carriers of
Divine Light
So let us live...happiness and peace to each other...is what
we need
to give.
And, spread calmness...spread love...let us accompany
each like hand
in glove... Accompany each other like hand in glove.

Chapter. 14. Roshni

The Sun is surely is going down behind those trees...it is definitely about to set,
It is about hide behind that endless horizon...where the skies and
the earth have already met.
Tomorrow, however, when it comes back...when it springs
back into sight,
It shall bring along with it...a new hope...it shall bring back all of
that beautiful light.
For, it shall end all of that unending darkness...it shall show
us all a new and brilliant ways,
It shall grant us all its energy...it shall bless us with its love...its
ethereal golden rays.
It shall help us lift our soul...it shall make us stand up whenever we fall,
It shall bring an end to all of our negativities...no matter

how big

or how small.

And, in the end...it shall ask us all to transform

ourselves...to

change our very heart,

To stop us in our mundane tracks...to inculcate a fresh

and a

positive start...........................

..............................To stop us all in our... ohh.... so

mundane

tracks and inculcate a fresher and an even more

energetic start.

Chapter. 15. Unlove

When I am no longer of this world...that moment,
when I stop breathing and die,
Come to my grave...is what I request...at least give it a
try.
When you see me for the last time, tears shall be shed by
your
beautiful eyes,
As and when you see my sepulchre lying still and cold...
pointing towards those cloud filled skies.
My love for you shall never end...even when I have
passed on,
I shall always be in front of you,
Into all the elements that make up this universe...I shall
forever
blend.
I shall watch over you...I shall be your be your star,
I shall always be by your side...I promise you, I shall
never wander
too far.
I shall talk to you when you talk...shall walk with you

when you
walk,
I shall be to you what a blackboard is to a chalk.
So, come over and meet me at my grave...once in a while,
Share that beautiful smile of yours...brilliant and awe
inspiring as
the river Nile.
Tell me that you love me...end my eternal pain,
So that I may rise from that grave and live again.

Chapter. 16. Us

Let us all be branches...channels to spread this beautiful light,
It is, in all of its awesomeness...
a beautiful sight. This light has finally arrived...
to take away all of our pain,
And, along with it all those unending negativities...
that were driving us insane. So...let this light shine...let it last,
For, there are many a beautiful people...many a familiar faces...
Yet...we find our hearts filled with a feeling of hatred...
a feeling of being alienated from one another.
He made us and called us, "Mankind"...but, not even an ounce of
kindness left inside of us. The thing is, we might be good human
beings...but, how good are we at being human??!!

Chapter. 17. Woh Log

There are so many people...so many faces...as many as
there can
be,
Yet...I feel alone, lost and ignored...I am a being that none
of
them can see.
There is a lot of ruckus...a lot of noise that I can very well
hear,
Yet...I am surprised that I am totally invisible to them
all...given
the fact that I am standing in front of them...I am quite
near.
They're ohh so busy with their own petty, mechanical
and surprisingly
cold lives,
Friends roaming around with their friends, mothers
taking care of
their children and husbands trying to please their wives.
They take their existence for granted...as if they knew
that they

were meant to be,
Their arrogance is so strong and so piercing...it is the
only thing I
can feel...and the only thing that I see.
Thanking and praising God...well...to them it seems out
of place
where and when they work,
To them a person who praises Him...is a big fat jerk.
His House...it seems, is merely utilised by them to
acquire free of
cost food and water,
The hymns of His Name...the peace and tranquillity of
that Holy
Place...has been replaced by their ignorant laughter.
They have forgotten that He exists...He has been reduced
to an
image or for that matter a painting on that dirty wall,
Going to His House...therefore, has become nothing
more than a
mundane routine...that is all.
Well...I shan't countenance the attitude of these very
individuals
anymore,
I shall continue to praise Him...His work and His
presence without
fail...to the hilt...and, to a very beautiful galore.
For me His Light shall always keep shining...in the form

of the

mighty Sun,

All the elements of Mother Nature...I shall treat them as gift...a

blessing that is second to none.

And...alas...when I leave this mortal form...the day when I die,

I shall meet Him...talk to Him...I shall seek an answer to all my

questions...no matter how hard I may have to try.

I shall fold my hands...ask for forgiveness and thank Him for

giving me my soul,

I shall ask Him to keep me with me...absorb me in Him and never

let me go...therefore, making me complete...making me whole.

Chapter. 18. Gratitude

"It has been told time and again...that we have yet to come across that can remotely qualify as a good read, Well...I can assure you of continuous e orts to give you all that you have been looking for. Yes!! Turned every rock... every stone...I have indeed!
However for those with insatiable palettes...craving for more!! Well...do not fret!!! For, this is just a start...or should I say...a couple of millions good starts,
For, this isn't the end...no my dears...'Pratibimb' shall have innumerable avatars...it shall go on with numerous chapters comprised in those unending parts!
So, until then...make sure that your wishes and blessing never ever end,
And in return for your beautiful emotions...loads of love and hugs through these very lines and these pictures...I shall continue to send!!

Light Up the Darkness."

www.ingramcontent.com/pod-product-compliance
Lightning Source LLC
LaVergne TN
LVHW022030200926
848481LV00007B/2620
* 9 7 9 8 8 9 8 6 5 7 4 1 3 *